RECORD BREAKERS

MEGASTRUCTURES

DAVID JEFFERIS

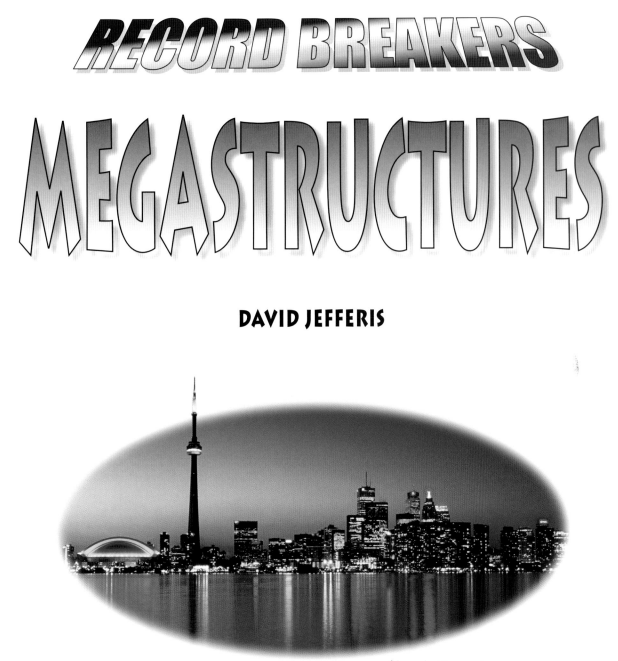

RAINTREE
STECK-VAUGHN
PUBLISHERS

A Harcourt Company

Austin   New York
www.raintreesteckvaughn.com

Published by Raintree Steck-Vaughn Publishers, an imprint of Steck-Vaughn Company.

Library of Congress Cataloging-in-Publication Data is available upon request

ISBN 0-7398-6324-X

Acknowledgments
We wish to thank the following individuals and organizations for their assistance and for supplying material from their collections:
Alpha Archive, British Airports Authority, Burj al Arab hotel, Richard A Cooke, CRD Photo, Corbis Images, Richard Cummins, Disney Enterprises Inc.,
Eden Project, Ericsson Telephones, Eurotunnel Plc, Golden Gate Bridge Highway and Transportation District, Hong Kong International Airport, Jawoc/EMPICS Sports Photo Agency, National Space Center, Cesar Pelli and Associates, Galen Rowell, J Sainsbury Plc, Thames Barrier/Environment Agency, Simon Warren, West Edmonton Mall, Michael S Yamashita.

Diagrams by Gavin Page
Project modeling by Emily Stapleton-Jefferis
Educational advisor Julie Stapleton

We have checked the records in this book but new ones are often added.

Printed in Taiwan. Bound in the United States.

1 2 3 4 5 6 7 8 9 0 07 06 05 04 03 02

▲ The Taj Mahal, built between 1632–1647, is the most famous megastructure in India. It is the tomb of an Indian princess and her husband.

Previous page: The CN Tower in Toronto, Canada. At just over 1,814 feet (553 m), it is the world's highest building.

CONTENTS

 LOOK FOR THE MEGASTRUCTURE SYMBOL

Look for the stadium building in boxes like this.

Here you will find extra facts and records.

BUILDING BIG

Megastructures are the giants of construction. People have been making them for thousands of years.

▲ The purpose of Silbury Hill is unknown, though one legend says that the forgotten King Zel is buried there. The Hill is around 131 feet (40 m) high.

The earliest megastructures were built about 5,000 years ago. These were often earth mounds, though why many were built is a mystery. In Europe, Silbury Hill in Great Britain is the largest mound, which we think was built about the same time as Egypt's Great Pyramid. We do know exactly what season work started. Remains of winged ants have been found deep in the foundations, and these insects appear only in late summer.

▶ The Great Pyramid was made from about 2.3 million blocks of stone, each weighing over 2.2 tons.

▼ The Great Wall of China was started in 221 B.C., but sections were added for centuries after. It is the world's longest structure, at about 2,150 miles (3,460 km) long. There are also many extra branching sections.

The earliest known stone megastructures are the pyramids of Egypt. The Great Pyramid of Giza was built around 2940 B.C., to house the body of the pharaoh Khufu. It is the tallest pyramid ever—when built, it stood 482 feet (147 m) high.

FIRST MEGASTRUCTURES TIMELINE

The pyramid of Kukulkan in Mexico is 89.9 feet (27.4 m) high.

2778 B.C. The Step Pyramid of Zoser at Saqqara, Egypt, is the first pyramid built.

2700 B.C. Work starts at Silbury Hill in Britain.

2700 B.C. The Great Pyramid is built at Giza in Egypt.

221 B.C. Work starts on the Great Wall of China. At first it is mainly earth and rubble. Later, stone walls are built.

A.D. 700–1200 The Maya and Toltec peoples of South and Central America build pyramid temples.

▲ The steel Gateway Arch is a recent monument. It is the tallest in the United States, at just over 630 feet (192 m). It was finished in 1965 and was designed to last 1,000 years.

MONUMENTS

Whether they are made of ancient stone or modern steel and concrete, monuments are all built to last a very long time.

Stonehenge in Great Britain is one of the world's most famous ancient structures. The circle of stones that stands today was raised about 1500 B.C., though earlier structures were built on the same site long before this.

Building Stonehenge was a huge job, since there were no machines to do the heavy work. Some of the stones came from a site in Wales, nearly 249 miles (400 km) away. Experts think that they were dragged over land on long wooden rollers and floated across rivers on big rafts.

▼ The biggest stones at Stonehenge weigh about 55 tons (50 tonnes). They were hauled into place by up to 500 people pulling on leather ropes.

A stone placed across two upright stones is called a lintel.

MONUMENTS OLD AND NEW

1500 B.C. Stonehenge is built in Britain. Other early structures include those at Karnac in France and on the island of Menorca in the Mediterranean.

A.D. 1000 The Moai people of Easter Island in the Pacific Ocean start making statues, until about 1500. The biggest is left unfinished. If it had been put up, it would have stood nearly 72 feet (22 m) high.

1965 The Gateway Arch opens in St. Louis, Missouri. It is a monument to the pioneers who opened up the "Wild West" in the 1800s.

some Moai statues are just a head and shoulders, but others have a body

▶ Hundreds of the mysterious Moai statues were carved from "tuff," a type of stony volcanic ash. They were placed in the open, overlooking Moai villages. They are thought to be connected to ancestor worship.

statues range in size from 7–43 feet (2–13 m)

REACH FOR THE SKY

New materials and building methods mean that today's towers and skyscrapers can reach higher and higher. But older towers are still amazing.

▲ The Petronas Towers in Kuala Lumpur, Malaysia, became the world's tallest office buildings in 1998, with a height of 1,483 feet (452 m).

The most famous tower of all is probably the Leaning Tower of Pisa in Italy. It was started in 1173 but soon began to lean because the ground underneath was not stable. There were many ideas to stop it from falling, but it was only in 2001 that engineers finished work that made it secure.

Today's towers are much taller, and engineers have to take even greater care with foundations.

▶ New York's 1,453-feet (443-m)-high Empire State Building opened in 1931. It was the world's highest building for many years.

the Eiffel Tower was built only for an exhibition but was so popular that it was not taken down when the show closed

TALLER AND TALLER

1887–1889 The 984-feet high (300-m-high) Eiffel Tower is built in Paris, France.

1976 The CN Tower in Toronto, Canada, opens. It is the world's tallest visitor attraction, at just over 1,814 feet (553 m).

1996 The Commerzbank in Frankfurt, Germany, is Europe's tallest building. It is 984 feet (300 m), including the radio antenna.

▲ At 1,509 feet (460 m) high, the Chinese Shanghai Tower's design is a little taller than the Petronas Towers. There are plans for even higher structures in the near future, to be built in Russia and India.

◄ The Leaning Tower of Pisa was closed in the 1990s for fear it would collapse. It is now open to visitors again—but going up a tilted tower is a weird experience!

▶ The Space Needle broke records for its sky-high revolving restaurant when it was built for the 1962 World Fair in Seattle, Washington.

the top of Space Needle is 604 feet (184 m) high

GIANT CASTLES

Castles were first built to control the territory around them. But some newer ones have been built just for their appearance and are used as royal homes.

▲ This fairy-tale castle is the most famous in Germany. The Schloss Neuschwanstein was built as a palace for King Ludwig of Bavaria.

Castles were built on high ground to dominate land nearby. This might be an important town or country that needed protection. Many castles were built in Europe and the Middle East. But the use of gunpowder ended the age of the military castle, because even the thickest walls could be destroyed with explosives.

MEGASTRUCTURES FOR KINGS AND QUEENS

A.D. 880 Work starts on Prague Castle in the Czech Republic. The world's biggest castle is still used by the Czech government.

1080 Windsor Castle is started by William the Conqueror. The first part built is an earth mound. Later, the Round Tower is built on top.

1869 Work starts on Schloss Neuschwanstein in Germany. Carvings in the king's bedroom take 14 carpenters over four years to complete.

► The top of Windsor Castle's Round Tower is more than 213 feet (65 m) above the country around it, which gave soldiers a good all-around view.

▼ Windsor Castle has stone walls, a cannon on display, and many stone carvings. The buildings show how styles have changed over the years.

Windsor Castle near London is the world's largest castle used as a home. It belongs to Queen Elizabeth II. The castle was built over 900 years ago as one of a chain of forts to protect London. The castle was extended many times and eventually covered an area of 13 acres (5.26 hectares).

stone beasts like these are called gargoyles

CHURCHES AND TEMPLES

▲ The temple at Abu Simbel in Egypt was built for the pharaoh Rameses II. The statues by the entrance are 69 ft (21m) high.

Many of the world's biggest buildings were made for worship. Some of them have survived to the present day.

The 3,300-year-old Abu Simbel Temple is in Egypt, overlooking the Nile River. In the 1960s a dam was built across the Nile. As the waters rose to form Lake Nasser, Abu Simbel could have been flooded. But in a race against time, engineers and scientists took the temple apart and rebuilt it more than 197 feet (60 m) higher!

The Parthenon is the most famous Greek temple. Much of it has survived, but a carved frieze around the top is missing—it was taken away many years ago to display in England.

◀ The Parthenon is over 2,400 years old, but it still stands over the city of Athens, on a flat-topped rock called the Acropolis.

BUILDING FOR WORSHIP

1270 B.C. The temple of Abu Simbel is built in Egypt. It is aligned so that, once a year, a ray of sunlight lights up statues of gods placed inside.

447–432 B.C. The Parthenon is erected overlooking Athens in Greece. It is built to worship Athena, the goddess of wisdom.

A.D. 537 Hagia Sophia is built in Istanbul, Turkey. Its huge 102-feet (31-m)-span dome is the biggest in the world for hundreds of years, until the 15th century.

1561 St. Basil's Cathedral in Moscow, Russia, opens. The big church has taken a total of only six years to build.

▲ Hagia Sophia is the biggest mosque in Turkey. The inside is covered in intricate decorations.

each spire is the roof of a separate chapel in the cathedral

▼ The colored domes and fairy-tale looks of St. Basil's Cathedral in Moscow make it the most famous building in Russia. It was built during the reign of the cruel czar, Ivan the Terrible.

onion-shaped domes are painted in bright colors

BIG DOMES

In the past, domes were mostly built on churches and cathedrals. Today's giants range from greenhouses to sports stadiums.

The domes below form the biggest greenhouse in the world, called the Eden Project. The huge domes (called biomes) are built in an old clay pit in Cornwall, England. Inside, visitors walk in environments created to be like real-life jungles and the warm Mediterranean area.

▲▼ The main domes of the Eden Project have a rain forest type of environment, with flowers, trees, streams, and waterfalls.

the dome has room for 43,000 people

the soccer field floats into the dome in about two hours

▲ The silver dome was built in Sapporo, Japan. It was made for the 2002 World Cup soccer finals.

This is probably the most clever sports dome in the world. The problem was that grass does not grow well under cover. So engineers built a soccer field that can move indoors when needed for matches. The field floats into the dome on an air cushion, like a hovercraft!

🏟 BUILDING A GREENHOUSE

Eden's domes are made of six-sided frames, bolted together. The windows are made of a lightweight plastic that weighs 100 times less than glass.

Building Eden was a big job—the pit is as large as 35 soccer fields, and garbage trucks hauled away 2 million tons of soil.

The scaffold used was also huge—it used some 46,000 poles and 230 miles (370 km) of tubing.

the biggest dome is as high as a stack of 20 big trucks

FUN AND GAMES

▲ The Colosseum still stands in Rome. Here some visitors are circled to show its huge scale. The walls are more than 131 feet (40 m) high.

Megastructures aren't always built for serious uses. The ones on these pages were made purely for entertainment.

The huge Colosseum in Rome was opened in A.D. 80 for public events. Up to 50,000 people watched bloody games in which gladiators fought each other or killed wild animals brought in especially for the occasion.

Today the biggest fun megastructures are at theme parks. The most popular theme park is Disneyworld. In 2000 about 16.5 million visitors went there. It is not the oldest amusement park, though—this is thought to be at Bakken in Denmark, which first opened in 1583!

This dome is at EPCOT. Visitors can ride in monorails.

DISNEY, THE THEME PARK PIONEER

1955 Disneyland, in California, is the first big theme park. The thrill ride "Matterhorn Mountain" opens in 1959.

1971 Walt Disney World opens in Florida. The site's area is vast—twice the size of Manhattan.

1982 Disney's futuristic EPCOT theme park opens in Florida.

1983 Disneyland Tokyo opens in Japan. In 2001 it is joined by DisneySea, which has a water theme.

1992 EuroDisney opens near Paris in France.

◀ Roller coasters come in two main types—wooden, like the one shown here, and steel. The fastest coaster of 2000 was the Japanese "Steel Dragon," which hurtled along at nearly 93 mph (150 km/h).

it takes about 30 minutes to go once around the Eye

▶ The London Eye is the world's biggest ferris wheel, at 443 feet (135 m) high. It was built to celebrate the millennium in 2000.

▼ An Audi car was parked in one of the Eye's 25-person compartments in 2001. The idea was a publicity stunt, to show how little the car weighed.

SHOPPING ZONE

Once upon a time, going shopping meant a trip to the corner store. Today, it's more likely to be a supermarket or shopping mall.

▲ The GUM department store was Russia's biggest shop. It opened in 1895 and helped protect shoppers from the icy chill of Russian winters. Today it is a mall with many different shops.

Big shopping malls attract shoppers, but some companies mix sales with helping the environment. The world's most eco-friendly supermarket is in Greenwich, England. The store uses only half the energy of a normal building, helped by grass-covered earth banks that keep it warm in winter and cool in summer.

▲ Grass-covered banks on each side of the store help keep its temperature even, throughout the year. In the parking lot, wind turbines and solar power provide electricity for lights at night.

Dirty water from the store is filtered through reed beds until it is clean.

▲ The mall has a full-size copy of the *Santa Maria* ship used by Christoper Columbus.

West Edmonton Mall in Canada tops the world's shopping malls. Apart from 800 shops and 110 eating places, the mall has many other features. These include hotels, a dolphin lagoon, and the world's largest indoor water park. There are also four working submarines in the lake!

SHOP UNTIL YOU DROP

1877 Galleria Vittorio Emanuele opens in Milan, Italy. It is the world's first shopping mall, with open spaces and cafes under cover from bad weather.

1895 GUM (State Universal Store) is built on same premise as Milan.

1981 West Edmonton Mall opens, with 220 stores. By 2001 it is twice as big and has 580 more places to shop.

1999 The world's most eco-friendly supermarket opens for business in Greenwich, England.

▼ The Galleria in Milan is the most popular meeting place in the city.

HOUSES AND HOTELS

Only a very few homes are big enough to be called megastructures. But hotels are different, and some of the biggest are very grand indeed.

▲ The San Simeon castle in California was the world's most expensive house in 1939. The owner, William Hearst, paid over $30 million.

The tallest hotel is the Burj al Arab tower in Dubai. Most hotels believe five stars is the height of luxury, but this one has *seven* stars. The coldest hotel has to be the Ice Hotel in Sweden. It is carved out of snow and ice!

The biggest hotel of all is the MGM Grand in Las Vegas, Nevada. It has 5,005 rooms, as well as shops, pools, theaters, nightclubs, and casinos.

▲ The Ice Hotel in Sweden has been open to visitors since 1989. Every winter a new and bigger ice hotel is built, but by the next spring it has melted again.

MGM GRAND, THE MEGA HOTEL

93 elevators in the hotel's four towers.

3,700 gaming machines in the hotel's casinos.

5,005 guest rooms in the hotel.

18,000 doorways in the hotel.

30,000 meals are prepared every day. Guests and visitors eat 4.4 million doughnuts a year.

MGM Grand's towers are over 279 feet (85 m) high

hotel's lobby area

bedroom

health club pool

the hotel's shape is like the sail of a traditional Arab dhow boat

▶ The 1994 Burj al Arab tower in Dubai is the world's tallest hotel. It is 1,053 feet (321 m) high, and is built on an artificial island. At night the hotel is flooded with color from 142 lights.

BRIDGES AND TUNNELS

Bridges and tunnels were built as far back as Roman times. Today they are bigger and longer than ever before.

▲ The longest underwater railway is the Eurotunnel linking England and France. There are actually three tunnels—one each way for the trains and a smaller service tunnel between them.

The world's longest tunnel links the Japanese islands of Honshu and Hokkaido. This Seikan train tunnel is 177 feet (54 km) long. The Eurotunnel between Britain and France is only 164 feet (50 km) but more of it is underwater, at 24 miles (39 km).

The Laerdal Tunnel, between Bergen and Oslo in Norway, is the longest road tunnel, running for 15.2 miles (24.5 km).

Sydney's sail-shaped Opera House is near Harbor Bridge

▲ The 1997 Tsing Ma Bridge in Hong Kong is the world's longest road-and-rail suspension bridge, with a span of 4,518 feet (1377 m).

The bridge is nicknamed the "coathanger" by locals. Can you guess why?

◀ Sydney Harbor Bridge in Australia has the widest deck of any bridge. It is 161 feet (49 m) across, with eight traffic lanes, bicycle and train tracks, and a footpath.

DEEPER AND LONGER

1779 The Iron Bridge is erected over the Severn River in England. It is 102 feet (31 m) long and is the world's first metal bridge.

1937 The Golden Gate Bridge in San Francisco, California, is finished. The 4,199-feet (1,280-m)-span bridge remains the world's longest for 27 years. The bridge is painted orange, not gold, and is named not for its color, but for the Golden Gate Strait.

1994 Eurotunnel is opened. It links England and France.

1998 The Akashi-Kaikyo Bridge opens in Japan. This is the world's longest suspension bridge, with a main span of 6,532 feet (1991 m).

GOING PLACES

▲ In 1946 Heathrow Airport opened, with a row of tents instead of a passenger terminal.

Megastructures for travel include airports, seaports, canals, railways, and highway systems. They share one aim—to help travelers on their way.

The world's busiest airport is Hartsfield in Atlanta. In 2000 about 80 million passengers used it. Outside the United States, the busiest airport is London's Heathrow, with over 64 million passengers a year.

▲ Aircraft from dozens of countries fly into and out of Heathrow. There are about 1,250 flights every day.

Roads are also record breakers. Experts believe there are over 3.7 million miles (6 million km) of highway in the United States! But the world's *widest* road is in Brazil. In 1960 the Monumental Axis was opened to traffic in the country's capital, Brasilia. The Axis has only six lanes, but they cover a width of 820 feet (250 m).

◀ Heathrow's lost-and-found office takes in about 20 cell phones every day. Cleaners have even found a case of dead fish and a glass eye!

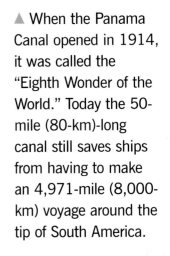

▲ When the Panama Canal opened in 1914, it was called the "Eighth Wonder of the World." Today the 50-mile (80-km)-long canal still saves ships from having to make an 4,971-mile (8,000-km) voyage around the tip of South America.

▲ The highways of California have the world's most complex junctions. One of them has a total of 34 lanes. More than 600,000 vehicles pass through this junction every day.

CANALS, ROADS, AND PORTS

1859 Work starts on the Suez Canal, linking the Indian Ocean with the Mediterranean Sea.

1914 The Panama Canal is finished and opens for ships.

1986 The world's longest city-bordering (ring) road is finished. The M25 makes a 121.5-mile (195.5-km) route around London.

1998 The world's busiest seaport is Rotterdam in the Netherlands, with over 358 million tons (325 million tonnes) of cargo.

1998 Hong Kong International Airport opens. Its passenger terminal is a record 4,167 feet (1.27 km) long.

MEGASTRUCTURE RECORDS

▲ The VAB is so big an entire space shuttle can be assembled in it. The doors are on the left.

Here are some facts and records from the world of megastructures.

OPEN UP!

The world's biggest doors are on the huge Vehicle Assembly Building (VAB) in Cape Canaveral, Florida. There are four doors, and each one is 456 feet (139 m) high. The VAB is used to prepare spacecraft for flight, and was originally built for the Apollo Moon missions of the 1960s and 1970s.

IT'S A LONG ROAD

The Pan-American Highway is the world's longest road. It goes from Alaska to Brazil, a distance of more than 15,000 miles (24,000 km). However, you cannot drive straight through—there is a gap in Central America.

CARHENGE

A henge (the word for any circular monument) does not have to be made of stone. In 1987 the Reinders family built a henge made of cars! Carhenge has 38 cars laid out like England's Stonehenge and all painted gray. Carhenge is in Nebraska, and gets about 80,000 visitors a year.

BIGGEST PALACES

The Sultan of Brunei owns the world's biggest palace. It has a total of 1,788 rooms!

In China the old Imperial Palace in Beijing covers an area of 178 acres (72 ha). It was started in the 1400s, but much work has been done since then.

DANGER — HIGH TIDE!

The Thames Barrier near London, England, is the world's largest movable river-defense system. It was built to stop London from being flooded during high tides. The Netherlands has a longer sea barrier. The 6-mile (9-km)-long Oosterscheldedam has 62 floodgates.

◄ London is protected by the Thames Barrier. When an extra-high tide is due, massive gates swing up to stop seawater from surging upriver to London.

◀ The biggest terminal building is at Hong Kong International Airport. To help people move around, there are 70 moving walkways and a shuttle train. The airport was built on an artificial island, as there was no room for it on the mainland.

SUPER SQUARE

The world's biggest public square is in China. Tiananmen Square is 2,887 feet (880 m) wide by 1,640 feet (500 m) deep, which is enough room to hold a million people. Despite the square's huge size, no one is allowed to ride a bicycle—only pedestrians are allowed there.

PARKING THE CAR

The West Edmonton Mall in Canada is not only the world's biggest shopping mall, but also boasts the largest parking

▼ Tiananmen Square is the world's largest square and Beijing's top visitor attraction.

lot. There are spaces for over 20,000 vehicles. The mall is the size of 48 city blocks. If you want to watch a movie, there's a choice of 26 theaters. After that, you might like to try splashing around in the world's largest indoor water park.

MEGASTRUCTURE WORDS

Here are some words used in this book that you may not know.

CZAR (ZAR)

The title used by the rulers of Russia until 1917. Can also be spelled "tsar."

FOUNDATIONS (FOUN-DAY-SHUHNS)

The base on which a structure rests, usually concrete. Steel rods are sometimes sunk into underlying rock.

FRIEZE (FREEZ)

A decoration forming a band around a room or a building. The Parthenon in Greece had a stone frieze around the top.

GARGOYLE (GAR-GOIL)

A small stone creature on the side of a building. Churches often feature them as waterspouts. Rainwater runs off the roof and out of the gargoyle's mouth.

GLADIATOR (GLAD-EE-AY-TOR)

In ancient Rome a person who fought other people or animals at a public show, often to the death. Special arenas, called amphitheaters, were built for the purpose, like the Colosseum in Rome.

HENGE (HENJ)

A circular monument, often with an outer raised earth bank or a sunken ditch.

HOVERCRAFT (HUHV-UR-KRAFT)

◀ These big apartment blocks were built on solid rock, a strong foundation. A structure built on softer ground may need a thick concrete base for safety.

A form of transportation that has no wheels. Instead, it has fans that blow a powerful cushion of air underneath, so the hovercraft floats just above the ground or water.

LINTEL (LINT-UHL)

The crosspiece across the top of a door or over a window. In Stonehenge, lintel stones are laid on top of two uprights.

MONUMENT (MON-YUH-MUHNT)

A structure built to last a very long time, often to mark an important event or person.

MOSQUE (MOSK)

A temple for people of the Muslim faith.

PASSENGER TERMINAL (PASS-UHN-JUR TUR-MUH-NUHL)

The building at an air- or seaport where travelers check in. Most terminals also have shops and restaurants.

◀ The Golden Gate is one of the world's most famous suspension bridges. Over 116,000 vehicles use the bridge's six traffic lanes every day.

PHARAOH (FAIR-oh)
The title used by the rulers of ancient Egypt.

RING ROAD (RING ROHD)
A highway that goes around a town or city, so that vehicles can avoid the center. Ring roads help cities avoid traffic congestion and pollution.

SANTA MARIA (SAN-tuh MUH-REE-UH)
One of the three ships used by explorer Christopher Columbus when he sailed from Spain to America in 1492.

SOLAR POWER (SOH-lur POU-ur)
A machine that can extract the energy from sunlight. Some solar systems use the sun's heat to warm water. Other systems can convert the energy in light to electricity.

STRAIT (STRAYT)
A narrow waterway that links two larger bodies of water.

SUSPENSION BRIDGE (SUH-SPEND-shuhn BRIJ)
A bridge that is supported by cables from large towers and anchored at each end.

THEME PARK (THEEM PARK)
An entertainment complex that has one main theme or idea. For example, Disney's EPCOT (Experimental Prototype Community of Tomorrow) was built to show off futuristic ideas and plans.

TUFF (TUHF)
Rock made of volcanic ash. As the ash builds up, its weight squashes the lowest layers to form the tuff. It was used for the statues of Easter Island.

WIND TURBINE (WIND TUR-buhn)
Any modern machine that extracts energy from the wind.

WORLD FAIR
Exhibitions held in cities around the world, where countries display their culture and achievements.

MEGASTRUCTURE PROJECTS

These experiments show building methods for early structures.

It seems amazing that early peoples could have built a megastructure like the Great Pyramid. At 482 feet (147 m) high, it was the tallest human-made object in the world for nearly 4,000 years.

There were no powerful machines at the time. Rollers, ramps, and levers were the main tools used, backed up with lots of muscle power.

◄ The Pyramids at Giza in Egypt were built using millions of cut stones. Each stone weighed several tons.

ROLLING STONES

This experiment shows how people in early civilizations could have moved heavy stones without using modern power equipment. They mostly avoided pushing heavy stones along the ground. They used rollers instead, which make the job easier.

1. You need round pencils (not with flat edges), a kitchen tile, and a weight such a can of food.

2. Place the can on the tile, and push the tile along. Feel how much effort you need.

LEVERS AND WEIGHTS

Levers are useful when lifting heavy weights. The balance point of a lever system is the key to its success. By moving it back and forth, you can make a heavy item easier to lift.

▲ Stones like these each weigh several tons.

balance point

balance point

1. Use a stiff board, a can of food, and a battery. Attach the can and battery with modeling clay where shown. Push down to lift the can.

2. Move the board to the halfway point over the battery. Now push down again. You will find the can lifts with much less effort.

3. Now lay the tile and can on the pencil rollers. You will find that they move far more easily than before.

4. To keep the tile and can moving, take out the back pencil and replace it underneath the front of the tile. You can move them as far as you want.

INDEX